Recipes for the Disaster

Gareth Sion Jenkins

© Gareth Sion Jenkins 2020

This book is copyright. Apart from any fair dealing for the purposes of study and research, criticism, review, or as otherwise permitted under the Copyright Act, no part may be reproduced by any process without written permission. Inquiries should be made to the publisher.

National Library of Australia
Cataloguing-in-Publications entry
Gareth Sion Jenkins
Recipes for the Disaster
ISBN: 978-0-6488079-4-0

Author photo: Natalya Shinn
Book design and cover image: Gareth Sion Jenkins
Typeset in Garamond: 10pt, 12pt.

Published by Apothecary Archive, July 2020
www.apothecaryarchive.com
Apothecary Archive operates on Gadigal land.

For the family ...

The full moon hovers over us
lifts us into the fold of its whole
        carries us
in the curve of its lap
                worn white-hot in the laid-out sky.

Contents

6   Cover

Blood

11   Blood bank
13   There'll always be music
14   A void in the windscreaming
18   The crossed roads
19   Mapping like all colonisers like to map
22   Fluid symmetry
23   Grand touring: morning feels forgotten
25   Darger in the undergrowth
26   The everywhere anywhere 1

Time

33   Time machines
38   Never the imposter
39   Life on earth
40   Grand touring: maybe the moon
42   I am
43   Dismantled by distance
44   This all over the earth
46   What would you rather?
48   Grand touring: that marina after Africa
49   Bees eat time
50   The Formulary, 1934
51   The everywhere anywhere 2

Dream

59 Dream sequence
61 On leaving
62 Recipes for the disaster
68 Without names
69 Swallows loudly
70 Grand touring: the exhibition
73 The point
74 Ferocious | Honey!
75 Landing
76 The everywhere anywhere 3

Cover

'It looks like a cross,' she said about the † at the top and it does look like that. 'I'm interested in the other meanings of letters,' I said. So it is a cross and it is a † like the cross down below that we drew on the manikin in 2003 that time because we couldn't get a real body—I can't remember why we didn't use our own bodies, which were real, even back then. In the cross that is not a cross that is a † I am running on Uluru/Ayers Rock which has been its dual/duel name since 2002 on the Northern Territory Government Place Names Register, changed from Ayers Rock/Uluru which was its official name since 1993, changed from Ayers Rock which was its official name since 1873, changed from Uluru which is its name—perhaps, me not being the one to say.

Anyway in the † that is a cross that is a † I'm running on Ayers Rock because it's 1983 and that's what I would have called it back then. I'd like to unrun those steps and unsay that name but I can't but I can at least be honest about taking/saying them. I'm not sure what that's worth but it's all I have to offer—

The colours are just colours because for a long time I only used black and white and then I started to use colour and liked it and used it here because they said the cover could be in colour.

The sewing affixes all materials and activates muscle memory from the past lives expressing themselves in my geometric DNA.

'Don't ever use gold,' she said, 'ever'—but she said this in my mind when I imagined showing it to her. Of course I had already used it by then, just a bit so perhaps she wouldn't see it and she didn't see it because I didn't show it to her because I thought she wouldn't like it. Then I'd wonder about changing it and I didn't want to change it because I liked it and then I did show her and she said, 'That looks better' and I said, 'Better than what?' and she said, 'I'm not going there' and why should she into that fragility.

After I thought about it I knew what she meant she meant better than the first time I showed her which was when it had only the central R shape. That R stands in for Recipes and underneath it are the first letters of all the other words in the book title For The Disaster and the letters are made out of film font which is how they used to make the credits in feature films. When I explained this she said, 'That doesn't mean anything to me' and even though at the time I said, 'So what?' I went straight away and put all the other letters on and the colours and the manikin cross and the scraps of receipts from my travels in India and the photographic negative my father took of me running on Uluru and she was right like I knew she would be—it does look better now.

Blood bank

1.
Compost mixed with old blood.

2.
A tide of blood. A porcelain cradle.

3.
Blood appears as a blanket laid down underneath.

4.
Your horse-head mask lying on the floor covered in blood.

5.
One more dose.
Absorbing the steady rhythm of your blood.

6.
Skull buzzing: blood   stream   love.

7.
Ambulance. Dark blood falls freely.
The liquid.

8.
Pain abates.
Blood into pristine.

9.

Unstable melodies in my blood.

10.

The back window. Latex gloves. Arms wiped free of blood.

11.

Material property: *spiritual flesh and blood ... the good virtue of the earth.*

12.

A trail of blood. The tracks of shoes.

13.

Covered in dried blood.

14.

A burst blood vessel moves away from me in all directions.

There'll always be music

On our first date she gets fired for selling me half-priced drinks.
She throws the beer in her boss' face and walks.
'He's lucky I didn't knife him,' she says
    'how am I going to pay my rent?'

I remember the knife shining on the counter
the one she used to slice lemons for vodka.

I look out the window at all that London going by.
I'm scared of her and utterly in love.

A year later I visit her in Denmark.
We sit in the piano room overlooking Ward Z.
'There'll always be music,' she tells me.
Leonard Cohen. She's translating him into Danish
with the writers' group she's formed in the asylum.

A single note from her finger against a key.
The grounds are filled with empty aviaries.
The ocean sweeps in towards a black pebbled beach.

A void in the windscreaming

1.

I mean: It is the impact of speaking to you again now you are dead.
Strands of hair against my skin and petrol fuming.   A hole
in the windscreen, your empty seat.   Blindness
after the oncoming light.
I mean: There was this accident.

2.

I wake with images in my fingers:
your bent shadowface within my prints.

Blood   a mirrored surface. Your reflection dries
into non being—are you listening?
I would sing to you but do not have the breath.

Would you listen then?

Move your eyes again?

3.

My heart is compressed chambers, flooded by collision:
desire for movement   at speed.
The bend came with rushing light
windscreen: last threshold   first flight
launch velocity   you parted glass
aperture for moon in   red blue   red blue   red blue lights
light my heart

    it is far too dark in here.

4.

A tire spinning against the blown-out sky.
Bright animals come with sand for this new ocean floor.
The sea withdrew tomorrow

                  took you.

5.

I mean: There was this accident.

Everyone woke up dead   not everyone woke up
dead   there were lots of dead.

I mean: Up side down fast sparks lifted
from my hair.   Up side down glass shifted   arms dangled
hands puffed   swollen with blood and head.

My head was full blood.

Too full blood in side out.   Too much blood out
came too much up side   down   me up side down you out side
down dead sheep eyes.

Are you listening?

I mean:

6.

Bright animals cut my frame
fuming stranded time
through a void in the windscreaming.

    Lured into space by gravitational pull
of bright moons   blatant scope of sky
irrepressible expansion
stars shed skin
across a car's underbelly:
exhaust   suspension   drive shaft.

7.

I orbit
are you listening?   I mean
                time
reflects off moving parts   relative perception
    light's receding

drive   exhaust   shaft   suspension

The crossed roads

Spotted gum skinned bark drifts
red-brown of kangaroo tail
hardwood terraced floor sanded lacquered back.

Speckled-brown of egg shell
orange-red-brown of hot coal smacked clean of black
blonde-brown of sandstone sediment.

Mustard-brown of kitchen Perspex splashback
orange-brown of that Mini Cooper S burning Bridge St nearly airborne
through the crossed roads.

A thousand thousand years
these roads been trailing—crossing
green-brown with moss holes bored perfect precision drill bits
been through there.

Mapping like all colonisers like to map

Red-tailed black cockatoos
perched in low scrub around Lake Woytchugga
sound off like an old car door being slammed.

In that expanse of jigsawed mud
a palm-sized anchor
clutch of small pharmaceutical bottles
crab claws—
edges worn white smooth
pincer hinges still working.

Local teens taking us to their favourite spots
mapping memories on our GPS
teaching Luisa how to say Woytchugga
till I can't recognise her voice on the DAT.
Teaching me how to get mobile reception in the desert
    that to pick up a black feather here is to invite a visit
from the Feather-foot
    come journeying to unfaithful men for revenging.

The sound of rocks being dropped
    as the school bus starts up. I let the feather (foot) fall
from between my fingers   (what punishment
    for writing its name?)   cockatoos lift off.

Air-con at Jim's Motel drone-rattles a background
for the three-day drive it took to get here
still churning my mind.
The shower drips intermittently
in time with the whistling of kids cruising on BMXs
tires filled with dried reeds.

Another late-night visitor crunches over gravel
past the dog trap stocked with a roo leg to tempt the packs
that run down the corrugated back lanes
through to the Mallee.
I roll over to face the door.
Surely a Feather-foot would arrive without sound.

Outside a semi shifts into low gear
on the Barrier Highway doing Broken Hill—Wilcannia—
Cobar—Orange—Cobar—Wilcannia—Broken Hill—
desert-going tankers ploughing through town
past the Liberty where the lights stay on all night
diffused by thick clouds of mosquitoes
obscuring kids milling around the bus-stop shelter
                        chewing on time.

In the morning they take us to the bridge
another generation wanting to jump off
like that song says by The Wilcannia Mob
but only when the river is above the 50-cent
octagonal disk three quarters up the support pylons
and never on the town edge.   They wait on.

I imagine my grandfather crossing this bridge,
a line's foreman for the P.M.G. department servicing the far west:
Broken Hill to Cobar and back round the dirt through Menindee
post-WWII signalman settling desert country
tending wires without the distraction of shrapnel
new baby just home and him on the road   like me.
We never met but I see him camping out here in the shadowed scrub
khaki tarp draped off the back of his old van.

After the bridge last stop is the weir.
It's around here that Sir Thomas Mitchell forded
first white surveyor taking angles with his theodolite
marking distance with chains
mapping the passage of the Darling in blood   for violence to follow
my own steps a continuation of that short white line.

The boys take me closer to get a better look
up to our chests in river reeds soft as feathers
that deep green hive hums all my secrets
as the wind comes through.

    A pair of pelicans circle
    in a downward glide
legs dangling for the pleasure of it the drag and guide.
  Landing on the weir of chunked rocks
    they lift their wings into the sun.

Fluid symmetry

We met and meet again under blood-bone moon.

It was a distance   those jungle trails
tangling us in rarefied air
certainly   a distance
contracting.

The low wet canopy lifts me into fields
of you drifting among lengths of maize
the tip of your shoulder blade   so familiar
turning   cheek bone architecture
             a foregone conclusion against the wind.

Your clay-fired headscarf shot with mirror
    you radiate light
    fluid symmetry orchestrates our fragile reunion
on Kilimanjaro's glacial rim.

    We are so high up here
             bright curvature of sky.

Grand touring: morning feels forgotten

Hyenas stand on a mound in the savannah
eyes caught in light from our head-torches, flames of our fire
the crying of deranged dogs communicating in code:
    time to strike   time to wait   time to strike
    shifting paw to paw, thick shoulders swing narrow heads
    jaws vibrate, deep chittering of teeth and larynx.

Gavin's vomiting blood now
cerebral malaria seizing muscles
stiff neck, head at odd angles
ends of dreadlocks stained dark red.
We take turns talking him back from a coma.

Yesterday, when we met up again with our truck
he was still talking: snippets of Scottish T.V. shows
from his childhood, said Derek.
Gavin had just driven four days up the edge of Lake Malawi
through dense mosquito season.
We'd taken a boat where a man lay dead two days
    wrapped in a floral blanket
    dark hair visible at one end, pale creased soles at the other.
I'd taken a photo of him and didn't feel bad.

The boat where a gutted horse got hauled on deck
cut up with cleavers sold to passengers,
bloody bags of meat handed out until they ran out of bags
then just chunks, carried in hands
rested on steel surfaces
blood drying dark brown over worn rivets
on the last leg of that journey up Lake Malawi.

    It's a scene I've reimagined: that boat
navigating the lock into the marina, Owen in his horse-head mask
stolen ambulance waiting on the dock
inspired by London's Surrey Quays
where I will live on a barge with Liam after Africa.

    Gavin lies half inside, half outside the tent.
    The hyenas can smell blood.
    Derek is dosed up on Lariam and Malawi Gold.
    He's spent all our money and now we camp in the open
    thinking of whatever the hyenas are keeping at bay.

We take shifts with the fire.
We take shifts with Gavin.

Jade cuts aubergines, douses them with salt and lets them sweat.
Liam plays his trumpet
sound reverberation offering fragile protection
in the Zambian outlands.

'I don't like aubergines,' I say.
'You'll like mine,' she says.

Night is so long morning feels forgotten
light coming like an afterthought over the grasslands.
We leave Gavin at the closest town and carry on.

Darger in the undergrowth

The General is watching blood fly from all angles.
 A tornado is coming.
 It will take 6000 pages to tell itself.
 Its name is Sweetie Pie.

The

everywhere

anywhere

1

It's about Number—how it is everywhere anywhere, how it is anything everything. It's about that night Owen numbered my future, made me his radical-pair, his silvereye fascination. It's about transmigration. It starts on a road but ends in a bath, somehow.

It's about a concrete underpass and the torque of a small engine. Owen speaks electromagnetic vibration his voice so clear I don't remember a thing he said.

> Owen is my gunkMother.
> I'm his baby.
> By the end I always feel dead.

A crack opens in the membrane anticipation drains my cortex of blood—sends my skull buzzing. A cold edge, the sign reunited with flesh—pain kisses me swiftly. The plastic sheet of the gurney.

Owen's rice-paper lips against my cornea. Latex fingers: a sharp wedge pushing his presence in. Owen lives inside me radiating keynote geometry. I watch through my eyelids street light comets career overhead a trail of algebraic formulas sing with the flat thrum of tires on the rough road outside.

Owen's heptagonal voice spreads cavities in my mind flesh holes in my sky ridge. Owen is the voice inside a dark iris lips kiss my right eye from inside.

I drink his resonant word sounds. Liquid sand suspended air intake. A tongue turns in my mouth, speaks me like the voice of the dead soldiers he pulled from the river. Like the voice of the red man he painted each line a vital interruption in the veneer.

I scrutinise the integrity of my composition.

A pause in the road thrumming. A turning into an elsewhere in the everywhere anywhere. The sound of water slapping against. The scent of chemicals and ground iron. The swing of metal doors hinging open, hinging closed. The body's movement through uncertain space.

Owen's breath breathing in the corner eating shadows all around me with fingertips pulling at my throat. He seems very real now.

His hands small birds lifted to my eye sea weed green glass green weed sea throat see see see vermilion. Bird sounds vibrate under my tongue with in my nerves feathers smelling of compost and old blood.

A hole in my sky ridge opens my right eye—Owen has woven a fresh skin sack to carry us anywhere everywhere underthick airwater my bones grow moss.

Time machines

1.
In aching light
I stand for a long time thinking
    your small hand.

2.
Of another
I had held at some previous time
    though it is nothing I can put my tongue to.

3.
My personality at this time
say elusive at best
an annihilated jumble.

4.
The throbbing in my leg
becomes audible time.

5.
I slip in and out of consciousness.
At times when I open my eyes you are beside me.

6.

By this time your voice radiates menacing intensity.

7.

Disaster   you tell me.

If ever there was a time

when a little external structure was required.

8.

Sounds settled into a dull murmur.

By the time we are dressed they are completely silent.

9.

Swedenborg is explicit this time:

Steal an ambulance.

Wait for a signal at the marina.

10.

Over the clumped terrace houses

a pyramid flashes four times in the sky.

        Latex gloves.

11.
It is time.

12.
Did I love you enough
at the time?

13.
Lifted into warmth
that time on the barge
that may or may not.

14.
Pontoons.
There are not many boats moored this time of year
still fewer residents.　　　Just you.　　　Just I.

15.
Four is the heart's time sequence:
equal by equal.

16.
Some genetic paradigm
to reorient myself next time around.

17.
Through the lens
I study your boat for a long time
extrapolate your movements from the shifting hull.

18.
Stare at the ceiling through your eyes.
Hear your voice for the first time.

19.
For the first time
it is some time else.

20.
You laugh
this time as a baby might   all gums and drawn lips.
You walk away   a column.

21.
Channels I have calved
your mouth moves all the time
breath squeezing between lips in a repetitive   controlled gesture.

22.
You mumble   'Life can be hard sometimes
                        but I really quite like it.'

24.
Four times you have fallen through my fingers.

25.
In aching light
I stand for a long time thinking.

26.
Time is very big.

Never the imposter

A cicada's digital call   clatter of leaves
                                                mandala of leaves
    serrated edge   torn rift   tapered point
    curl of a crapped leaf
    leaf of shaking flame
                          red gum caught in that unstable light
pale leaf of lemon rind
    crescent moon through morning mist.

The sounds of mountain waking in this human silence
    free-fall of small stones
    droplets of water
                 night's accumulation.

The going in.
The coming out.
Dawn feet through damp grass
morning of waterfall   bird call
                    sun
striking the orbital nerve
            breath breathing the brain   the body
breathing the lines that lift us
into life   always before   behind
    carried lightly   carrying lightly
this breath   never the imposter.

Thrush of canopy static
                        spotted gums
                        ghosted by mist
    a host of birds   singing their tiny hinges
at different angles
different speeds.

Life on earth

Bulb of a child's eye.
The many-hinged parts of a bee
moving smoothly between grey-green leaves.
Slow hoverings through time
                          silent from this distance.

Grand touring: maybe the moon

We are driving all night to make the morning ferry across Lake Victoria
in an old WWII German transport.
Our driver's name is Gavin, a tattooed, dreadlocked
pot-smoking Scotsman
hiding out in Africa like some kind of modern-day Rimbaud.

Sometime during late afternoon we become lost
though no one will admit it.
The road contracts.
Night descends and brings torrential rain.
Tall grasses either side of the truck fall inward
under the weight of water.
Headlights on drenched stalks cast shadow-beings
scuttling onto slick-clay incline
loss of traction   ten tonnes ditching.

A river of clay.
That snapped drive shaft.
After we're done it is past midnight.
In fact here—a small pool of light from a gas lantern
Jade cuts, salts and fries the aubergines.
I do like them.

Somehow we make it up that hill
find the road again.
Perhaps the rain stopped.
Maybe the moon came out.

Anyway—we are driving all night
to make the morning ferry across Lake Victoria.
We miss it by fifteen minutes.
The ferry will sink and every passenger will drown, perhaps
we clean our teeth to its departing horn
clothes hanging off us
stiffened with clay.

I am

    just   a   groove

    for

    a needle

    to fall in

    to

    to run along

        make

        music

Dismantled by distance

The sky a double-bass cloudscape playing rain
wet channels cut in clay: how important a water-tank
echoes that red wheel barrow. Hay-bale spirals
horse-hair scrub, wild flowers arching hillside
no wire for rain to run off.

Voices unbroken by fences, dismantled by distance.
Words gather, familiar stones piling in pockets.
The phones are down. It will soon be Christmas.

This all over the earth

1.

Between towered clusters blue mesh for sun to through
onto concave concrete overpass
mirrored glass angled towards   away from everything.

Scaffolding scaffolded by steel triangles   white columns
welded to rectangular platforms
suspended sun dials
fire-wire beams red white against orange angled roofs
against   sky   blue.

Red mesh for light to through onto plastic orange girders
triangular edges
leaves too
closer   green light glowing   through and against.

Distant grass   bright and long dark with shadow.

Men reflecting yellow stripes moving over rubble   over compacted
stone
through drifting dirt
light as air.

White trucks spray water to keep dust down.

2.

Crosshatched scaffolding tunnels above green mesh
    before blue mesh
    rain drenched.

White-tipped steel bars herded together in columns
for standing on end
for burying in pits bored in granite
                by punch-running cranes.

Polymer supports
capped in plastic yellow spheres
    piles of soil
    dark with oil   dark with coal   orange with clay.

Hydraulics   the moving of everything:
upper sheave lower sheave jib hoist rope jib strut
jib back stay boom point hoist rope boom guy lines
steel-trussed arms.

Yellow pylons stacked white-red
fit-together barriers
poured full by streams of soil
rooftop cranes countered by cement blocks
accurate to the gram.

Semi-circle of trees   of grass field
lilac shipping container rivered with rust
blue arm angling from boxed-in white cabin
        so orange inside
        sun climbing the screen.

What would you rather?

for Amelie

Parallel beams of sandstone against blue morning
above the red rock river bed
rotors of helicopters hollow out clouds.

She says all the way up
'I want to jump'   'I want to push you off'
'I want to break my leg'
'I'm having thoughts about death
       I don't mind
       it doesn't make me worried   I like it
       just saying'
       she says   'Not another photo!'

She hums and sings   begs for chewing gum
bargains   cajoles   demands   says
'Don't be angry
I'm having those thoughts again
jump off
push you off
break a leg' just saying
she says   'What would you rather?
       Die or jump in there?'

In there is Montezuma's Well
water full of arsenic
full of giant leeches
toxins collected on its ten-thousand-year journey from over the hill.

I film ten seconds of the American flag flying over the ranger's hut
to add to all the other ten-second snippets I've been recording
to make some kind of statement about America or flags
that I still haven't made.

'So?' she says. Leaning on the railing.
'Not much of a choice,' I say.
'No,' she says leaning over the railing, 'I'm going to write about this
in my diary, how a girl jumps in and is saved by a boy
and they fall in love.
                How do you spell unconscious?'

Grand touring: that marina after Africa

Liam and I work nights at *The Daily Mail* packing plant
with illegal Russians we call The Cranes—
    earning pounds before joining the French Foreign Legion.
    They say they're not worried about the Frenchies.
    They say basic training in the Russian Army
        is being buried up to your neck in snow and left for dead.

Other travellers live in the marina. I meet Liva.
She's a bouncer at The Candy Bar in Soho.
We drink camomile tea and smoke hash
scored in the toilets at the packing plant
from a guy that carries blocks of it in a cock-pouch
cut to feel like a stiff dick in case he gets frisked by cops.

In winter the marina freezes. In spring three foxes drown.
Liam tries to save one but gets his thumb bitten.
The ambulance waits on dock flashing its lights.

Liva slips into visions of schizophrenia—
a knot of giant frogs thunder the pontoons.
I visit her in Aarhus, she's staying in Ward Z
surrounded by empty aviaries.
A black pebble beach keeps back the sea.

That's how I tell it
but really she'd been released by then.
We go only to return a book to their library.
We spend a week having awkward sex
in mid-summer's perpetual sunlight, then I leave.

And those aviaries are actually in Adelaide
at the abandoned Glenside Lunatic Asylum
where years later I will film a time-lapse sunrise
the shadow of that tree slowly blooming across manicured grass.

Bees eat time

Twin bells wrapped in strung-out sheets.
A pitched cliff imploding dark window holes
            clustered antennas chatter in a vibrating dawn
            bees eat time.

Ladders leak light
into frozen water, dark rungs
chained to the wall   her hand on his arm
heads folded in cobbled intimacy. Stones heavy with after.

The Formulary, 1934

How you can't help but say *Mix the Exsiccated Ferrous Sulphate*
in iambic pentameter.

How it's the phrase *Oil of Cinnamon*
that most clearly evokes the Zambezi night markets,
where men of twine roasted maize to the hiss of hurricane lanterns
and you spined your finger on that urchin.
Locals gathered—soaked it in kerosene—said
'If you survive the night you'll be okay.'

Still the black spot   still the pain
lingers like the aftertaste of Kumar's chai
Syrup of Quinine and Strychnine
he drugged you with to feed you jewels
stitched closed and sealed with wax kept all this time.

As he carried you out into that *Magnesia* night
clusters of children kissed your hands with feathered lips
the corpse of some kind of minor prince   their faces bowed
upturned
quickly into the dark.

The

everywhere

anywhere

2

It's about a bath in an old factory beside a marina on the outskirts of the everywhere anywhere. It's about the right eye and a radical-pair reunion. Electromagnetic flight paths of migration.

It's about Number—how it's a resonant skin that warp wraps the everything anything.

It's about that night Owen grabs me from the street corner drags me into the ambulance and drives me hanging his head out of the window vibrating a storm into the distance.

It's about that night Owen says   'It's time'

                    and all the Numbers in that.

His hair stands on end and mine too as I lie in the back strapped to a gurney. The ambulance has a police scanner tuned to the frequency of the police talking about looking for an ambulance so I think maybe this time someone will find me—but nobody ever does.

Owen's small like a small boy but strong like a big man. He's like the boy I saw that time behind the Cobb & Co. mail stop. There was this rotten piano beautifully out of tune round the back being played by a woman with a violin spine.

I walked away from all that down to a little pathetic stream and there was this boy there. I asked him what he was doing and he said he was dragging dead soldiers out of the river. He was sweating and kind of staggering under their weight. There was no body but him down there.

Owen is like that and that other boy in my art class, the one that painted the picture of the huge wave and the tiny surfer and a shadow beneath it all. He said the tiny surfer was him. I said, 'Is the shadow a whale?' He said he didn't know what the shadow was but his cold sores did.

The next week he painted another picture, all in red. It had a man in it looking through a telescope and he left a big empty circle in the sky and said, 'Next week I'll fill that in so you know what he's been watching.'

Owen is like that boy, too. Powerful and jittery like an electric storm coming in over a marina on the outskirts of the everywhere anywhere making waves in the everything anything.

After we have driven we come to the factory and the factory is a lot like the factory I visited once with the performance collective Shagging Julie. We were going to use it in a show about Owen but then we didn't, because we didn't do the show because we couldn't get any money to do it. Owen puts me in a porcelain bathtub and I keep the bathtub company and he says:

> 'We are only lifted briefly from sequence into breath. A disturbance in the infinite resonance.' He repeats this over and over and won't shut up so I can't sleep.

Wind currents blast waves in earth's magnetic fields. The sea has risen. Owen's brought in the tide and with it a whale from out deep, circling in the marina singing bass obliteration.

Owen looks out the window. 'I've got this whale now but I don't know what to do with it.' Owen always has problems with motivation. That's because he is really just a kid down by the river collecting bodies and a painter covering canvases in red—Owen has never made any sense but I just can't seem to give up on him. Fourteen years now—we're like some kind of radical-pair, oscillating. We're like migratory birds guided by the magnetoreceptors in our right eyes.

The day is clouded with rain. Street lamps stay on. Their hum accompanies the everything anything, a harmony crying the whale circling in the storm singing the sharp edge of vibration. The meagre resistance of skin. In side out side claw at one another. Owen's a map on my retina visionary surface of the mind. I am a break in a smooth arc of porcelain. I breathe lightly. The earth a giant magnet guiding us home.

Dream sequence

1.
Hours:
her image inhabits my dreams. A variety of scenarios.

2.
I dreamed I attended an exhibition.
Hundreds of photographs soaking up the moisture on my skin.

3.
Entry: A void in the dream.
A hole in the sky ridge.

4.
It is not the first time I've dreamed of that last hour with Swedenborg or her gift of the Formulary.

5.
Dream language
is the beginning. Motivation must be strong. Wind is dark.

6.
I do not dream of you anymore.

7.
Her dreams draw me into the marina.
Kept at arms length by her body.
She watches me   her eyes are every breach.

8.
'I thought you didn't dream about me anymore?'
The corners of your mouth rise up
'ferocious   honey!'

9.
Nothing more is required as we approach
the second dreaming.   Four flares in the east.

10.
She is the pendulum inspiring
dreaming thick-tricking the brain.

On leaving

I reach for you

touching your shoulder where your wing lies open

flattened   by skin

      night

rain

      the curious weight of our laughter.

Recipes for the disaster

1.

Concentrated Orange Flower Water
Oil of Lavender

Your sensitive hand *ensures clear air way with mouth gag and tongue forceps*. You wield such implements with a causal violence, a *depressed head. Oxygen and artificial respiration* are required as I wake into the *Cardiac* dawn *and* breathe with the aid of *respiratory stimulants—intravenous coramine or adrenaline—intracardiac adrenaline.*

You line the barge with shadows the shape of fingers dripping *Tincture of Myrrh* into fragile hinges with which to *massage* open the peeled chambers *of* my *heart.*

2.

Spirit of Chloroform
Hard and Soft Paraffin

Within me I sense a tension residing in the bow-drawn swing of your arms: doors toward your *Oil of Lavender* abdomen. Now *Adrenaline,* your hands *applying it* to my chambers *by means of a thin glass rod ... dipped alternately into the Acid and the Alcoholic solution.*

The Alcoholic solution.

I hold onto this rod

glass thin singing with the effort of maintaining its form.

3.

Tincture of Myrrh
Garlic, fresh, peeled and bruised

See *the mixture of Oleic Acid and Spirit in a porcelain dish, stirring and warming* one another—evaporation hovers like sirens. I no longer think of my body as solid; it is numerous pieces shifting in to out of solution—only the sirens remain constant and your hands mixing pharmaceutical concoctions. *To be applied by gentle massage* you say of the *Hard and Soft Paraffin* that cakes your fingers.

Am I to go to you now?

You speak only to the little blue book beside you on the *Chlorazol Fast Red* linoleum. A *Concentrated Orange Flower Water* dusk spreads through your barge.

4.

Concentrated Spirit of Chloroform
Stramonium

I stand at the end of your barge watching you wipe your hands clean, you close the blue formulary and move towards the fire, laying your clothes on the rack to warm.

You dress from the bottom up—boots first   pants   shirt.

Sirens—distant but approaching, seep through the gaps in the buildings, through the city's *sand-bath* façade.

There's music: Leonard Cohen.
You sing along
in a variety of languages
a jazz composite   blaring like trumpet.

5.

Sodium Sulphite
Oil of Geranium

Your voice unaccompanied in Denmark's 3 a.m. summer
dawn light pouring through a high window
Tincture of Belladonna pooling.

Your fingers against a piano in the music room: searching
keys ring out into the sallow morning. From the grounds the
swelling of trees with wind. The *Stramonium* silence of your
room in Ward Z.

Ward Z: in florescent corridors tubes of diagrammatic light
plastic covers so discoloured with dust and dead flies
they barely glow, silhouettes of decomposing
insects crawling into tiny annexed rooms
big enough for a bed and equipped with straps.

6.

Chlorazol Fast Red
Tincture of Belladonna

We stand beside the aviary at midnight
birds deranged by late summer's luminosity: 'It's a great
metaphor,' you say your fingers through the grill of this cage
within a cage within a cage.

The aviary is filthy: rotting seed and bird shit dissolves
into depressed concrete. The birds have retained their colour
but their songs lack melody.

I watch you walk the grounds away. This my disaster point.

A *Sodium Sulphite* dusk spreads *Oil of Geranium* light
through your hair.

Silence gathers and slackens in coiled strands.
You're not wearing your glasses,
      your naked face is full of shadows

      you begin to sing.

Without names

We took our bodies apart
sat without names. Your hollowed armpit
    taut tendons of your knee.

You watched me from under low eyelids
        crossed your self over my self
        neck feet
        belly
        breast   breast
        shin in step thigh
        our connection rose on relentless wind with tender bite.

The music ceased, leaving vibrations: the needle catching itself
every now
every then
with the static of suspension
    a crack   cusping
    reminding us how precarious our balance on this edge.

Swallows loudly

for Natalya

Swallows loudly in ancient architraves wake me
         diving onto cobbled stones washed each morning.

The motion of my mind towards you
lips bent   feeling no thing
no thing finds me
swallows loudly.

I remember every dream in which you sing
your voice a hedged rustling:
    aural snow drifting into the Pyrenees rift
    your breath moves me breathing
    breathe   breathe me in.

I remember every dream in which you say:
    'My heart is four chambers singing your name.'

Come stand with in me.
Watch the morning light bright with swallow's wings uncoiling.

Grand touring: the exhibition

Over the Ugandan border
towards mountain gorillas
through towering fields of maize.
Blood-bone moon rising low and huge
between long green ribbed leaves rattling in the wind like blades.

Night closes in
we stumble over indentations
left in fields by hooves of bulls that pulled the ploughs.
For two hours each fall we fear for our lives.

The maize breaks open. We pitch tents. We make fire.
Our only food is an onion.
We curse Derek into dreams.

In the morning maize from a local farmer
chased from his field by an old silverback
beating his chest with gnarled fist.
The gorilla returns, an armful of cobs.
Sits on the hill
nimbly stripping husks.

Light bends through a valley.
I take a photo of a narrow dirt road.
Jade weaves a small basket from thick husks of maize.
I sit. Our knees just touch.
'You can have it,' she says
'It's empty—but you can have it.'

That night we share a tent for the first time.
I tell her we will always be connected by a silver strand of light.
She says, 'God, that's corny.'
She says, 'No, you can't go down on me.'
Between kisses she tells me about her boyfriend.

Liam is listening from the next tent.
In the morning he asks if I was crying.

At midday, machetes and the trek.
After an hour gun shots. Guides say, 'Poachers'
and slide rifles off their backs.
Guides say, 'Be prepared for dead gorillas.'

After three hours through jungle we see them.
I extend my hand and guides say, 'Don't give!'
I can't retract and guides say, 'Don't make eye contact!'
I can't look away as the baby touches my fingers
with her own, soft like a human child's
and her mother charges
me into the undergrowth.

She sits off to the side
cradling her young, a deep red gash on her wrist.
My chin finally lowers towards my chest.
Overhead, giant fronds massive away the sky.

Even the peak of Kilimanjaro at sunrise
after all night walking the black frozen volcanic ash cone
through mist so high it's cloud
won't compare to this—Jade and I
say goodbye sitting in a car park gutter at Nairobi airport.

It's a year before we speak again.
Back in Sydney, I invite her to my exhibition.

She says, 'I didn't know you were a photographer.'
I say, 'Don't you remember all the photos I took
when we were in Africa?'

A long emptiness opens
as she realises who she is actually talking to
and hangs up.

The point

She plays a ruined piano
her back   the shape of a violin
   muscles rolling
notes evolving with every pressure—her neck lists
        breaching itself on the point of a hundred discarded breaths.

She plays three hours
   the curve of her spine as she dances her fingers
   sings
   her hands
   make half-forgotten movements
half-remembered signals
       decomposing   signs.

Ferocious | Honey!

Noise smolders into speech, the *inscape* of voice
sonic furnace hot enough to mold teeth as she reads
        Márgarét, áre you gríeving
big-bellied in the floral heat *Over Goldengrove unleaving?*
Syntax shaping our brain, patterning our *inscape* then
his words on her breath, soft tongue
there is a god in that poetry of the womb
    who better to speak to the unborn?   Born
    that ransacked night we drag ourselves ashore.
    Gasping at air. Covered in snow. The thrashing *Deutschland*
    broken back grinding the offshore sandbank.

An Osprey calls out the dead wailing of waves wearing stone
not wailing but laughing not laughing but singing
five nuns washed ashore from *The Wreck of the Deutschland*
the storm a receding horizon wind *white-fiery* seas *endragonèd*
five nuns laughing, *inscape* of drowning fresh on their tongues.
There is a god in that moment of surfacing
in sand their fingers trace a *body of lovely Death*
black habits steaming the sun.

The nuns stop tracing singing laughing wailing stop.
We couldn't bring them back for long, poetry of the womb?
We laugh amid the dunes   quietly
faith viscous adrift now—ferocious | honey!

A god in that down stroke
line of unlikely correspondence catching us in the thigh
there is a god in that we think in bruised syntax   not broken
but open inscaping spread of sound through flesh tongues of resonance
we find them with our fingers press press laugh maintain we think
maintain we say this *hard-hurled heart-fleshed moth-soft* tenderness.

Landing

Dreaming

    a home coming

    with land

that has no memory   of me.

The

everywhere

anywhere

3

It's about that night the whale sung the slow song of wind down. It's about how we are all woken only briefly from Number into breath. A minor disturbance in the vibration of the anything everything. A Number removed momentarily from sequence. It's about your keynote, your resonant frequency vibrating the bones of you into flight.

'I've called the birds.'

His voice. A beacon. A regular pulse in earth's spherical harmonics.

I think briefly of Number. There is only wOne Owen, but really there have always been two. Form bleeds through itself. I crawl over the porcelain rim amidst gravity. The whale finds my resonant frequency its hum the steady vibration of the metal walkway an extension of the building I wade through shades of atoms into night.

The sky is blistered by stars. I feel the melody of the spheres as they spin in space aware of minute fluctuations in tone. He holds the creature in his arms. The twitch of its talons. The spasm of its beak. Its frenetic dissolving heart. 'I am not a kid anymore.'

'I know, Owen.'

He places the bird's right eye over my right iris. The world's metallic frame deviates, photons morph symmetric patterns fluctuate in a magnetosensitive reorientation—a radical-pair reunion. Resonant sonic boom vibrates my keynote into waves of ultraviolet light: 370 to 565 nanometers in length. The world gets bright green, then the shade of nicotine on his fingers clicking in my face.

He's standing over me. Not a kid anymore—24 perhaps? Looks like he's made of wire and cigarette burns. Flexing the kind of muscle that comes from missing meals. He leans back on the pushie he's motorised with an old lawn mower engine. We watch others hooning across the parkland beside the falling down back fences of falling down houses.

They circle around and fly through the concrete underpass beside the storm water drain. An alco slips on a submerged shopping trolley trying to drag something onto the cement shore. He ends up awkwardly perched on the frame, a small stream laden with chip wrappers flowing around his shins. He used to sit up on the hill under the trees watching kids play in the carpark till the cops moved him on.

As the bikes pass their unmuffled engines vibrate my ear drums. They hang a finger at Owen and he laugh-yells, 'In your dreams—still not as fast as mine,' and then more softly, 'Gotta get the torque just right.' I think about Number. 'Owen, it's all …' 'Don't you fucken even.'

There's not a mystical bone in his body that hasn't been broken. He hates all this radical-pair reunion shit. Hates that I keep obsessing about the kid he never was.

'Anyway, I'm off.' His mates have stopped beside the bottlo to wait for him. Late afternoon light refracts off millions of tiny shards of broken glass on patchy asphalt. Silvereyes pick at fallen chips and spring rolls looking at each one with sideways heads. The boys flick bottle caps at them, they rise momentarily then settle again.

'You got a tenner?' I check my wallet and hand him a twenty. He stuffs it in his pocket and lifts his leg over the bike. 'You know it wasn't even a whale anyway, right?' He starts his engine and yells the rest through a cloud of greyblue smoke. 'It was a shark and when those bastards come for you there ain't no singing.' He releases the brakes and takes off.

In the concrete underpass the alco is waving me over. I ignore him and walk up to a road. There's a bus shelter with Troy 4 Stacey 4 Ever burnt into the perspex with a lighter. The last bus out leaves at 5.15 pm and I've missed it.

In the distance, on the outskirts of the everywhere anywhere I can see the factory and walk towards it. Hopefully the ambulance is still there—it was last time.

Acknowledgements

To Natalya Shinn: always believing—that colourist extraordinaire | Amelie Jenkins: your narrative drive—your quick wit | Sarah Jenkins: the humour—the memory | Roger and Eve that bedrock | Michael Aiken: that great originator | Jason Lam—that other kind of Doctor | The Useful Box | Kate Concannon that knife-wielding editor | Obsidian | Wojtek Krajewski's harmonics | Josh Mei-Ling Dubrau—that violin spine | the Traditional Owners of the land I write on: the Gadigal—the Barkindji—the Dharawal—the Anangu | Pharmakon | Anthony Mannix that Erotomanic | the many students: schools—libraries—youth centres—universities—prisons | the many Owens | Johanna Featherstone Unlocking | the Youth Curators—their inspiring enthusiasm | the invented instruments: the cow with hammers—the Tupperware waveform generator—the blind-eye organ that sounded as it drew—the spring thing | sound poetry broken into the guttural | letter into shape | Film Font backlit by LED lights speaking constellations | needle—paper—thread—those ancient, essential technologies | African outlands | the Surrey Quays marina | Square One Studios | Hill 60: WWII bunker chamber—deep concrete resonance of a vaulted cathedral buried underground—a vibrating tomb—the generator couldn't power the projector—the walls were black traps for our tongues—cold as iron in that midnight sea storm | Wilcannia's Darling | Wollongong: the beach where midnight art was performed—that house an old brothel where I met love and that other house—the condemned one of creation | the Claymore underpass near my hometown | the Apothecary Archive: archiving itself into existence in the cracks between creativity and constraint.

Particular thanks to my friend Michael Aiken for his many years of creative inspiration and collaboration.

Huge thanks to all the editors of publications that have published my creative output, including many of the poems in this collection: *Rattapallax* (US), *Mascara Literary Review*, *Cordite Poetry Review*, *Unlocked Anthology* (Red Room Poetry), *Tincture Journal*, *Rabbit Poetry Journal*, *The Drunken Boat* (US), *The Dangar Island Garbage Boat: Newcastle Poetry Prize Anthology*, *VLAK: Contemporary Poetics and the Arts*, *Flash Cove*, *Australian Poetry Anthology*, *Pink Cover Zine*, *The Clambake: Cuplet 2018 Anthology*, *The material poem: an e-anthology of text-based art & inter-media writing*, *The Last Vispo Anthology: Visual Poetry 1998–2008*.

Thanks to the original publisher of this book, Five Islands Press. I am indebted to them and editor Bella Li for supporting this project in its early stages and for improving it in its latter. After their print run sold out and they ceased to operate as a press Apothecary Archive released the new edition you are now reading with minor revisions.

Recipes for the Disaster co-won the Anne Elder Award: an annual award for the best sole-authored first book of poetry published in 2019. Thanks to Australian Poetry and the award judges Gig Ryan, Marcella Polain and Rae White.

Recipes was also shortlisted for the Mary Gilmore Award: for the best first book of poetry published in 2019. Thanks to the Association for the Study of Australian Literature and judges, David McCooey, Dan Disney and Jill Jones.

Notes

Blood bank
Italicised text is a quote from *The Way to Christ Discovered and Described* by Jakob Boehme (1775): 'spiritual flesh and blood ... the good virtue of the earth' p. 216.

Grand touring
The 'Grand touring' sequence of poems was, in earlier drafts, called 'White man travelling' (I still wonder if it should in fact be called this). The current title is a reference to the 17th-18th Century practice of the Grand Tour: the wealth, whiteness and male privilege / prejudice that typified that form of travelling also enabled my own.

The Formulary, 1934
All italicised texts are quotes from *The Australian and New Zealand Pharmaceutical Formulary A.P.F. Sixth Edition, 1934*: 'Mix the Exsiccated Ferrous Sulphate' p. 32; 'Syrup of Quinine and Strychnine' p. 81; 'Oil of Cinnamon' p. 66; 'Magnesia' p. 168. One day I may rewrite this poem more truthfully.

Ferocious | Honey!
All italicised texts are quotes from *Poems of Gerard Manley Hopkins*, edited with notes by Robert Bridges (London: Humphrey Milford, 1918): 'inscape' p. 97; 'Márgarét, áre you gríeving' p. 51; 'Over Goldengrove unleaving?' p. 51; 'The Wreck of the Deutschland' p. 11; 'white-fiery' p. 15; 'endragonèd' p. 20; 'body of lovely Death' p. 19; 'hard-hurled' p.22; 'heart-fleshed' p.22; 'moth-soft' p.20.

Recipes for the disaster
All italicised texts are quotes from *The Australian and New Zealand Pharmaceutical Formulary A.P.F. Sixth Edition, 1934*. In order of appearance, from the following pages in the original: pp. 83, 36, 171, 88, 171, 28, 92, 36, 63, 88, 79, 76, 92, 92, 164, 83, 50, 170, 56 35, 88, 61, 170, 164, 61, 35, 88. Elsewhere I've called this method of writing a Radical Midrash. A conventional Midrash seeks to create a commentary that reinforces the meaning of a source text. A Radical Midrash however, seeks to reveal the hidden meanings and narratives in a source text.

Biographical Note

Gareth lives in Sydney with Natalya Shinn and Amelie Jenkins. He has taught poetry and poetics in schools, youth centres, universities, libraries and prisons.

His masters in psychology was spent measuring the brain's frontal positive slow wave. His doctorate explored the schizophrenic writing and artmaking of Anthony Mannix. He is the editor of *The Toy of the Spirit*, the first book-length publication of Anthony's collected writings, published in 2019 by Puncher & Wattmann.

Gareth's poetry and theoretical work has been widely published. His poetry-film collaborations regularly screen at festivals around the world. He makes and exhibits text-based art at Square One Studios.

In 2020 Gareth founded the digital repository and publishing house Apothecary Archive. The archive contains Anthony Mannix's Being of Art (as opposed to his body of work). Gareth's sound works, artworks and film projects can also be found there.

www.ingramcontent.com/pod-product-compliance
Lightning Source LLC
Chambersburg PA
CBHW030303010526
44107CB00053B/1795